the SMART UNICORN

ACTIVITY BOOK

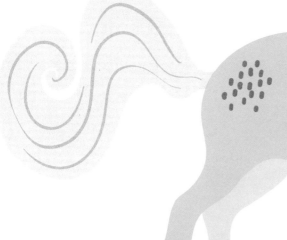

Magical Fun, Games, and Puzzles!

By Glenda Horne

CASTLE POINT BOOKS
NEW YORK

THE SMART UNICORN ACTIVITY BOOK. Copyright © 2020 by St. Martin's Press.
All rights reserved.
Printed in Canada.
For information, address St. Martin's Press,
120 Broadway, New York, NY 10271.

www.castlepointbooks.com

The Castle Point Books trademark is owned by Castle Point Publishing, LLC.
Castle Point books are published and distributed by St. Martin's Press.

ISBN 978-1-250-27491-5 (trade paperback)

Images used under license by Shutterstock.com

Our books may be purchased in bulk for promotional, educational, or business
use. Please contact your local bookseller or the Macmillan Corporate and
Premium Sales Department at 1-800-221-7945, extension 5442, or by email at
MacmillanSpecialMarkets@macmillan.com.

First Edition: 2020

10 9 8 7 6 5 4 3 2 1

THESE UNICORN DREAMS BELONG TO:

_____

COLOR

Copy the unicorn picture one square at a time!

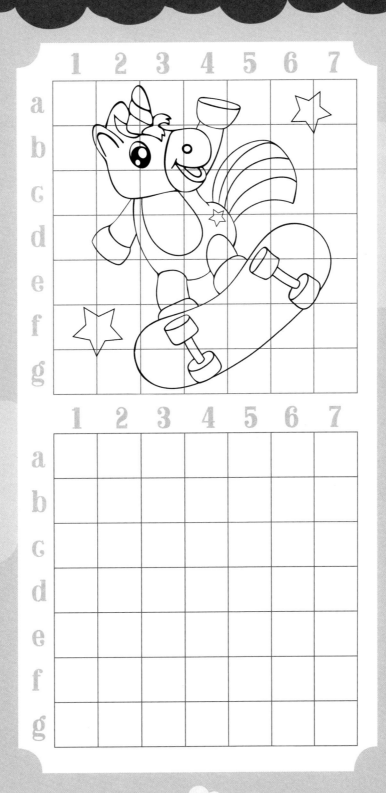

Can You Solve This?

🍩 + 🍩 + 🍩 = **21**

💎 + 🍩 + 🍩 = **19**

⭐ + 💎 + 🍩 = **16**

🍩 + 💎 − ⭐ = ⭕

⭐ + 🍩 − 💎 = ⭕

Crossword Animals

Match the image to the correct shadow.

Find the right path to the castle.

Write the missing letter.

ostrich

panda

mouse

rabbit

snowman

tiger

unicorn

van

walrus

xylophone

yacht

zoo

9

It's your fairy tale!

Write a story using at least 3 objects from the box.

_____

_____

_____

_____

_____

_____

_____

_____

_____

_____

Find 10 differences.

Copy the unicorn picture one square at a time!

Follow the path
by adding 3 to get to the gift!

33	21	19	3	21	19	34	5	31	8
21	7	8	16	17	34	15	37	40	🎁
1	4	6	8	12	30	30	34	25	17
1	16	13	4	7	16	14	17	3	28	31	5	19
21	14	31	14	10	13	16	19	22	25	33	36	38
23	27	30	21	27	35	31	21	24	25	26	27	38
19	3	25	15	21	26	2	12	2	1	33	31	30

COLOR

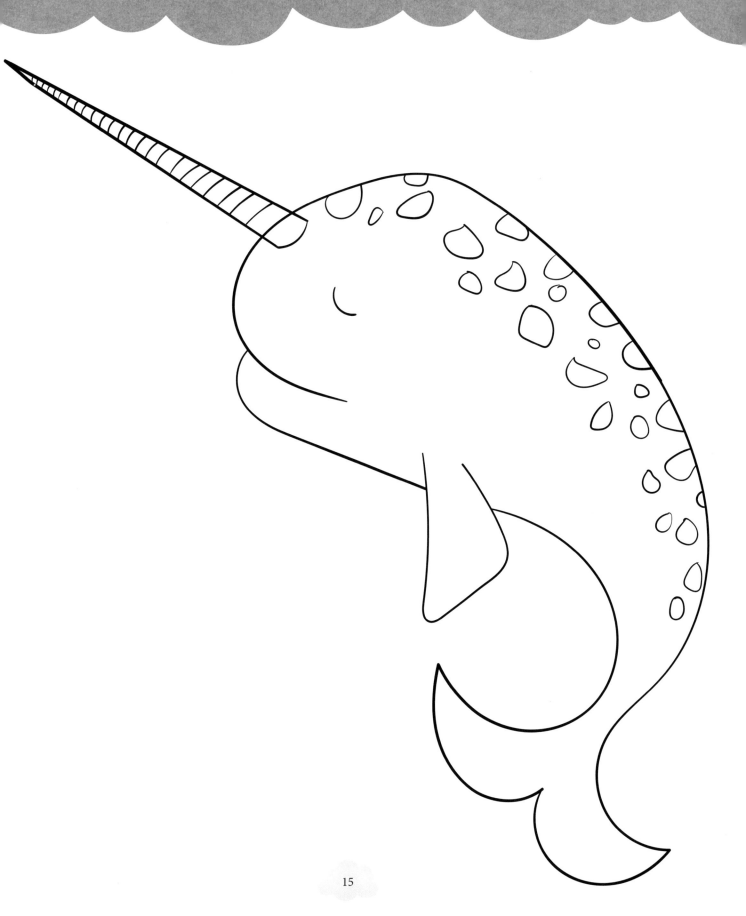

Follow the paths
to spell the word!

O C U N N I R

Follow the right path!

START

FINISH

Count the objects.

CUT and FOLD

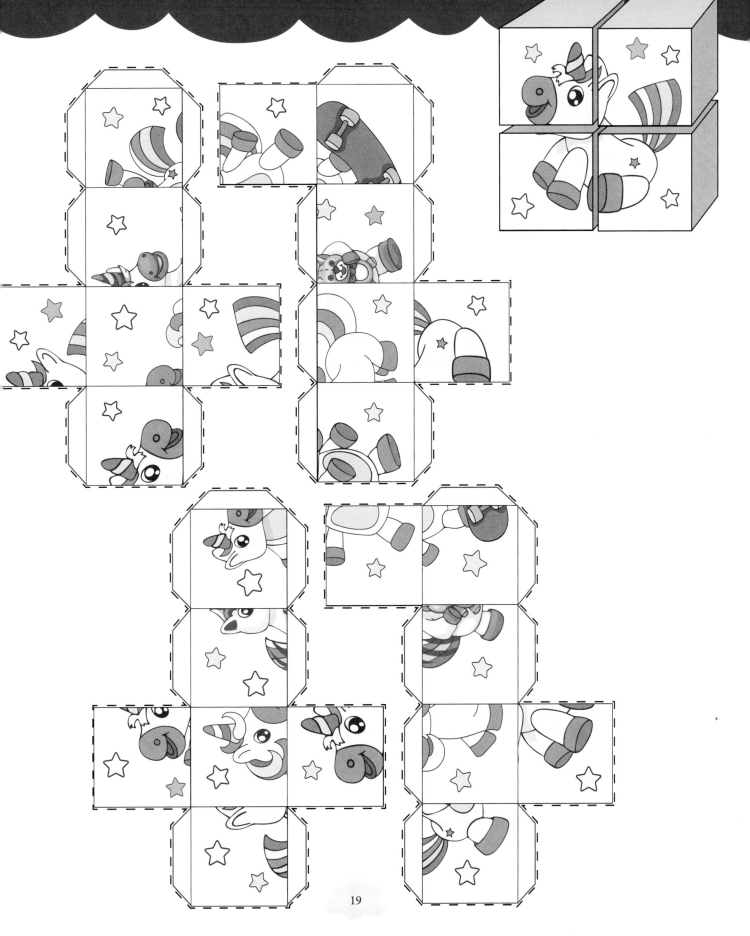

Find the right path!

CUT and GLUE

Cut and glue the image that comes next.

Solve the puzzle!

Unicorn Sudoku

Copy the narwhal picture one square at a time!

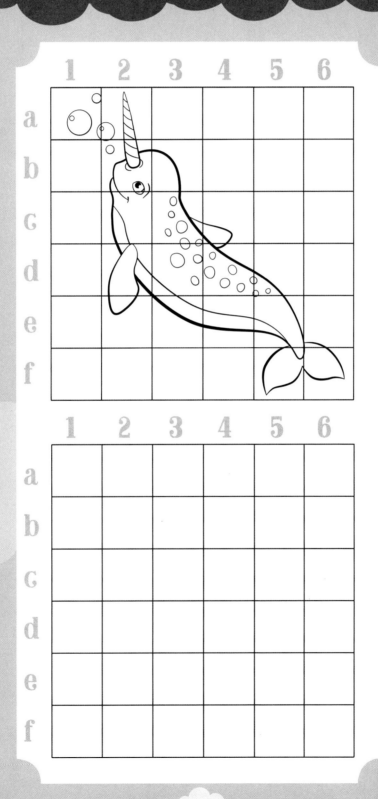

Count and match.

3	Five
10	Six
5	Three
4	Ten
6	Eight
2	Four
7	Nine
1	Two
8	Seven
9	One

Learn the alphabet.

Find the correct shadow.

Find 10 differences.

Count and match.

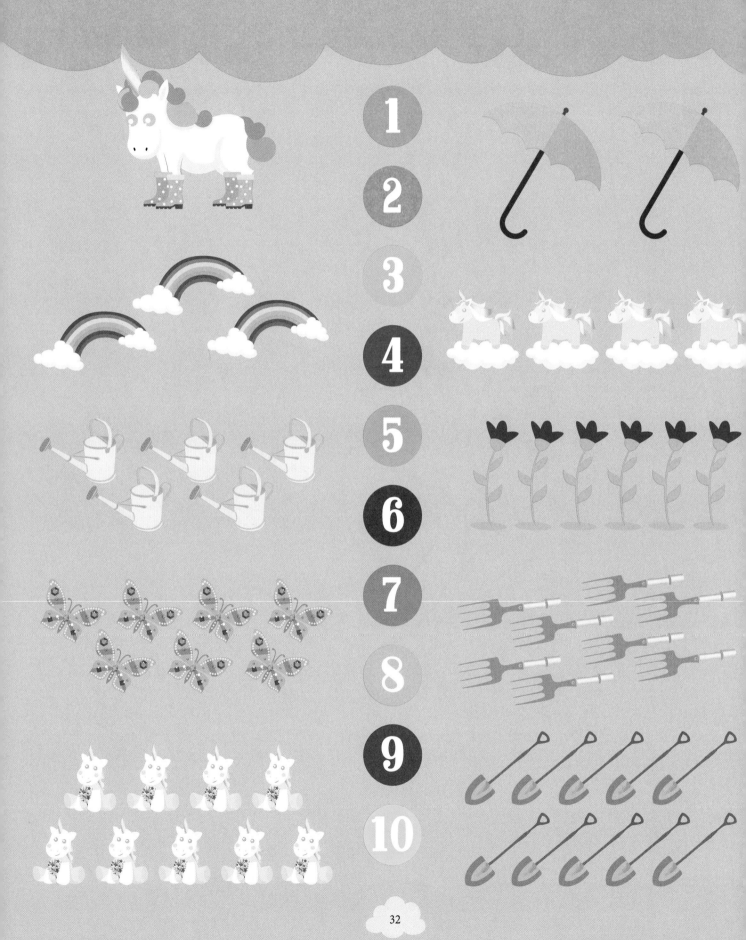

Find the right path!

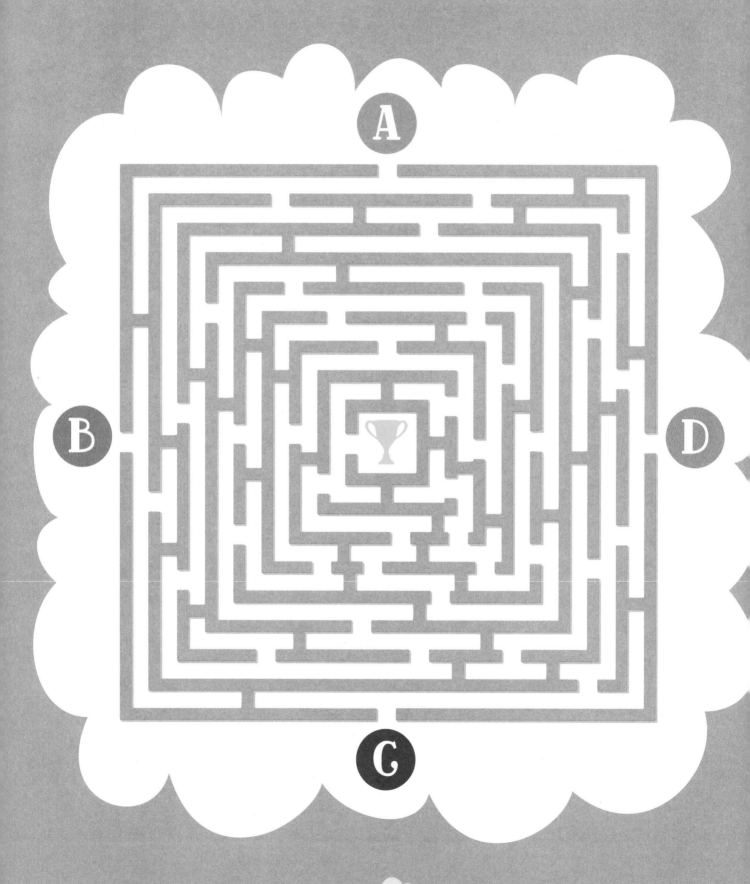

34

Play with numbers!

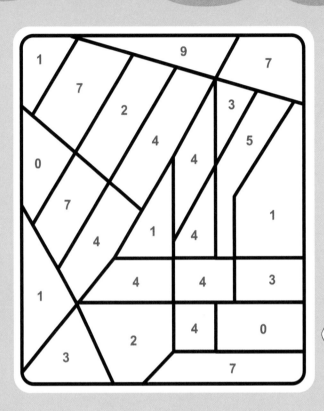

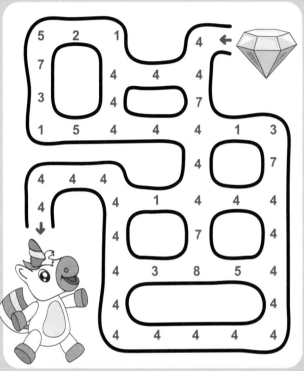

1   **2**   **3**   __   **5**   **6**   **7**   **8**   **9**

Color 4 porcupines

Draw 4 shapes

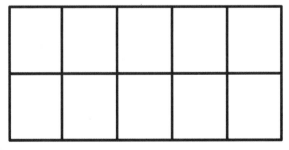

●● + ___ = **7**

▲▲▲▲ − ___ = **4**

■■■ + ___ = **3**

35

Unicorn Crossword

Find the right path!

How Many?

38

Prize-Winning Numbers

Match the numbers to the correct words.

1st	sixth
2nd	ninth
3rd	seventh
4th	second
5th	fifth
6th	first
7th	fourth
8th	third
9th	tenth
10th	eighth

Unicorn for a day!

If you were a unicorn for a day, what would you do?
Write about it here.

TIME
TO BE A
UNICORN

_____

_____

_____

_____

_____

_____

_____

_____

_____

_____

Copy the unicorn picture one square at a time!

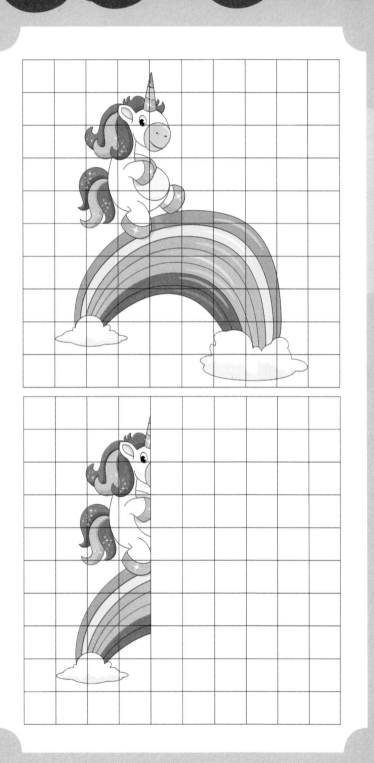

Connect the letters.

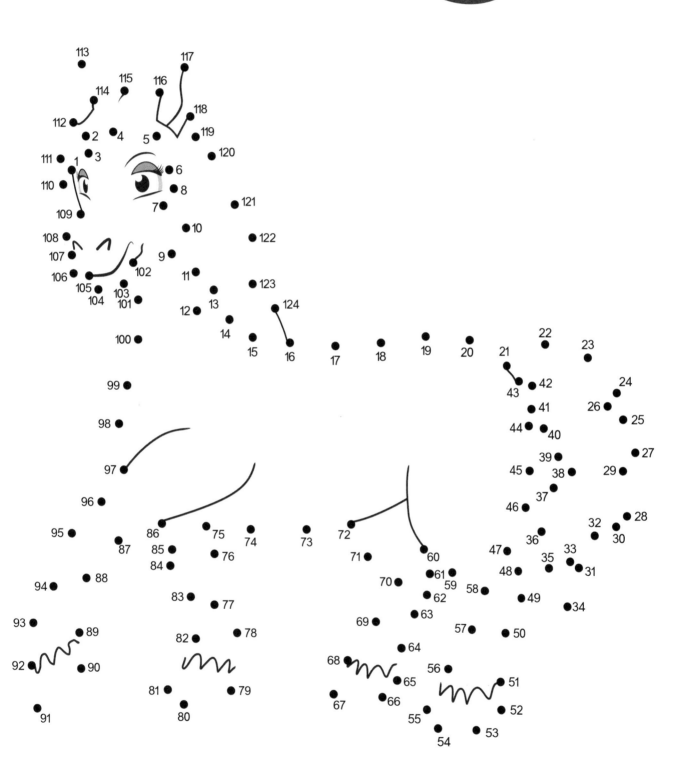

COLOR by SYMBOL

Find the Right Path!

Find the right path to the castle by following the numbers in order.

2	3	4	5	5	6
1	8	9	6	7	12
		15	16	8	18
		21	10	9	24
25	26	12	11	29	30
31	32	13	34		
37	15	14	40		
43	16	45	46	21	48
49	17	18	19	20	54

COLOR by NUMBER

Crossword
Animals

Find the right path to the cupcake by following the numbers in order.

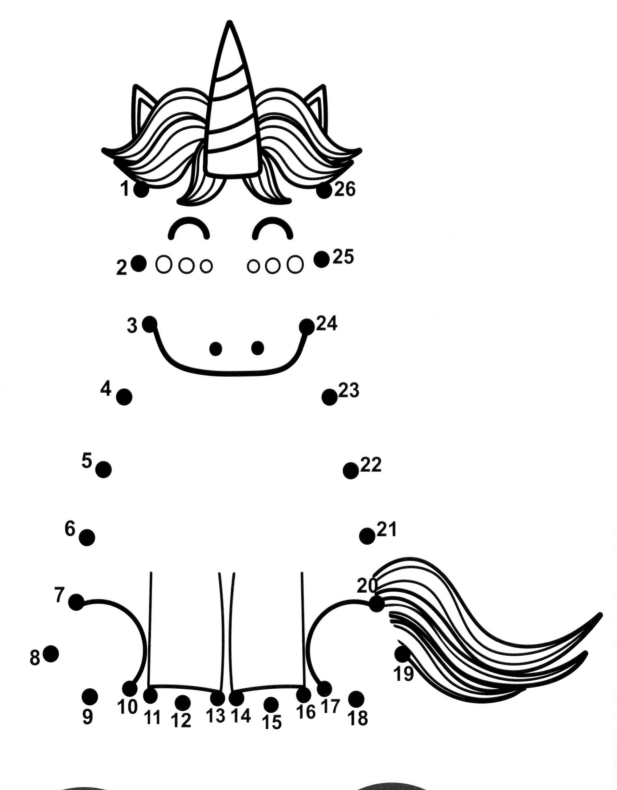

1
26
2
25
3
24
4
23
5
22
6
21
20
7
8
19
9 10 11 12 13 14 15 16 17 18

Find the right path!

Math Matching Game

1+3 10+4 15-5 2+9 8-4

4 11 10 14 4

Find the right path to reach the rainbow!

Find the right path!

Copy the picture
one square at a time!

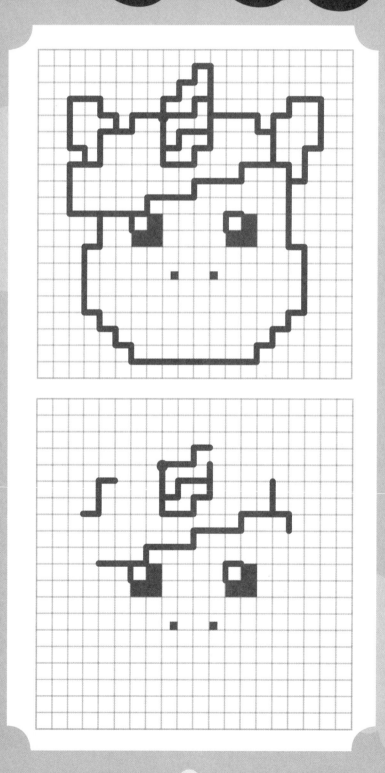

COUNT and COLOR

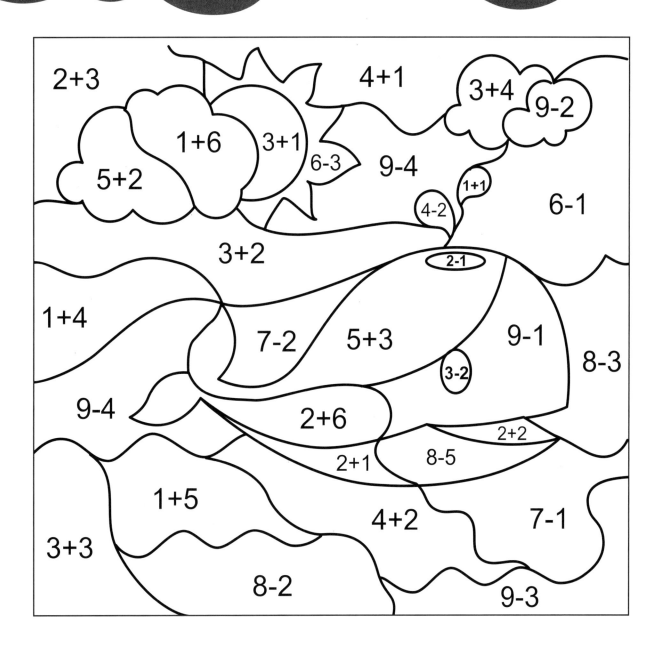

Greater than, less than, or equal to?

Uu

Unicorn

COLOR

and draw the hands on the clocks.

6:15

10:40

12:25

3:15

8:35

5:20

1:30

2:55

Find the right path!

Find the right path to the flower by following the numbers in order.

Counting Game

8 + 5 = ☐

10 − 8 = ☐

7 + 7 = ☐

8 − 7 = ☐

7 + 6 = ☐

Find the right path!

NUMBERS

0	0	0	0	0	0	0	0	0	0
1	1	1	1	1	1	1	1	1	1
2	2	2	2	2	2	2	2	2	2
3	3	3	3	3	3	3	3	3	3
4	4	4	4	4	4	4	4	4	4
5	5	5	5	5	5	5	5	5	5
6	6	6	6	6	6	6	6	6	6
7	7	7	7	7	7	7	7	7	7
8	8	8	8	8	8	8	8	8	8
9	9	9	9	9	9	9	9	9	9

Find the matching pair!

Can You Solve This?

$$5 + 5 = \boxed{}$$

$$5 - 2 = \boxed{}$$

$$2 + 1 = \boxed{}$$

CONNECT the DOTS

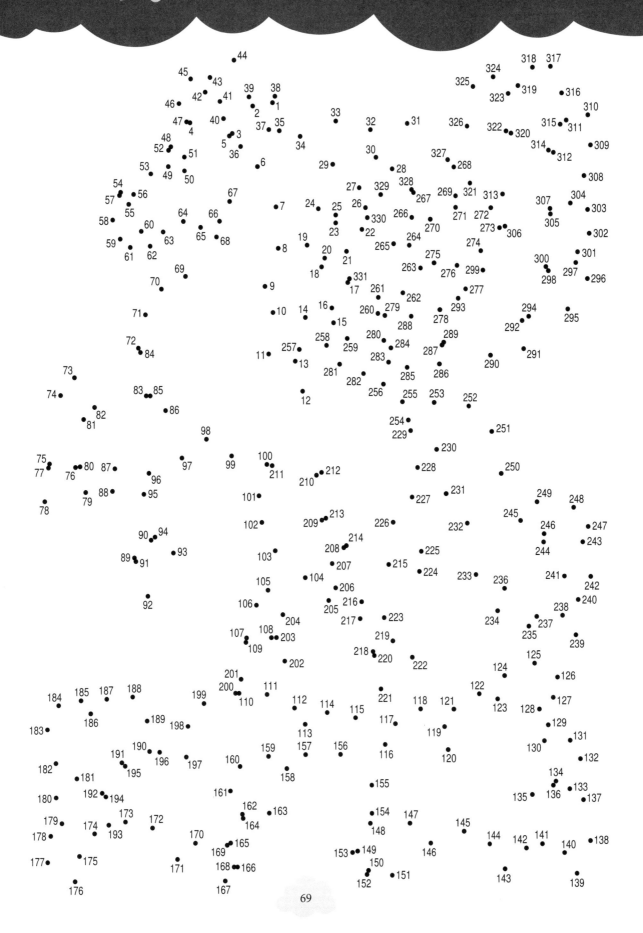

Find the right path!

Count the Money!

$10 + 5 \; 5 \; 1 \; 5 =$ ☐

$10 \; 20 - 2 \; 1 \; 5 =$ ☐

$20 \; 1 \; 5 + 5 \; 10 \; 1 =$ ☐

COLOR

and find the right path!

Find the right path to the rainbow by following the numbers in order.

Find the right path!

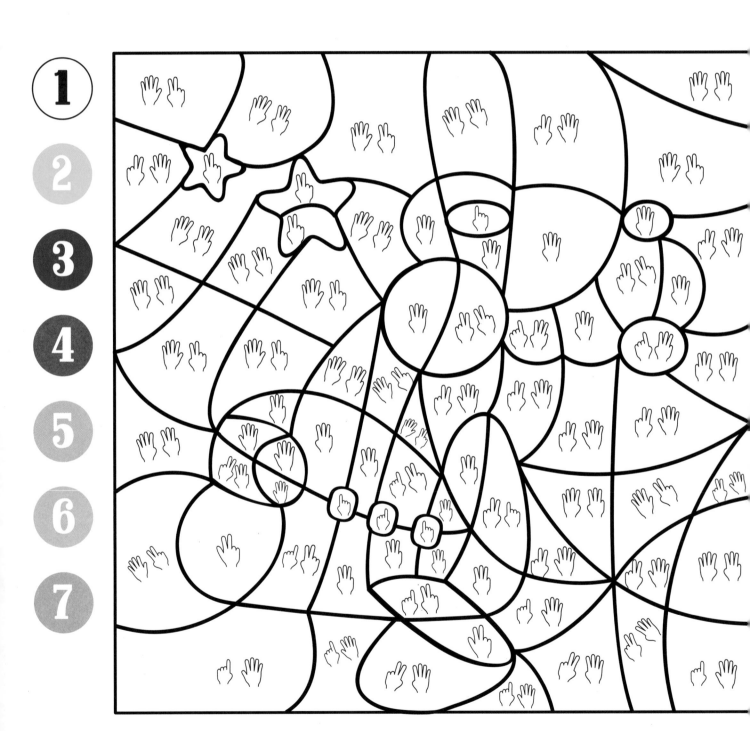

Find the right path to the honey!

CUT and GLUE

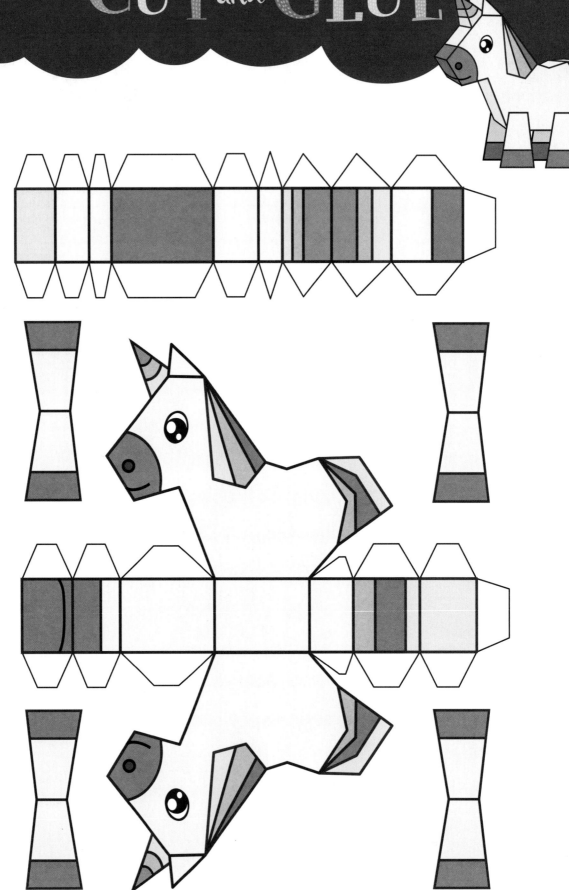

78

Find 10 differences.

Copy the unicorn picture one square at a time!

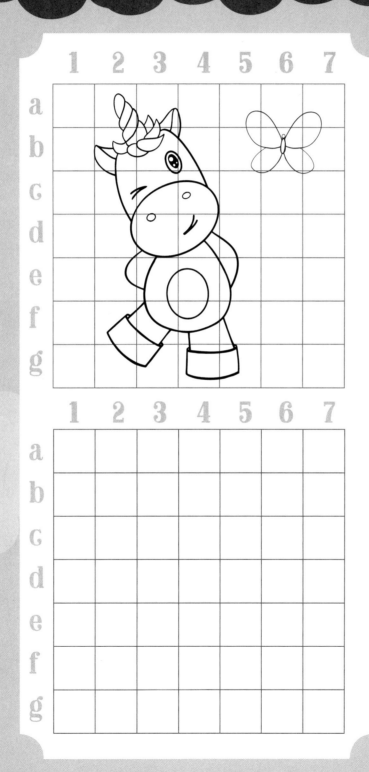

	1	2	3	4	5	6	7
a							
b							
c							
d							
e							
f							
g							

How Many?

Find the right path!

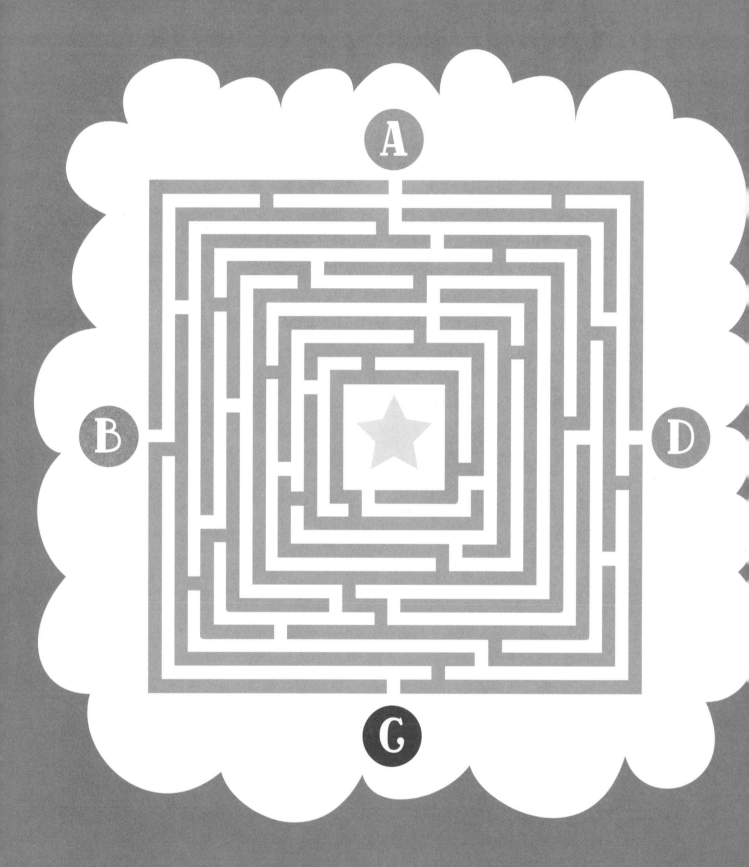

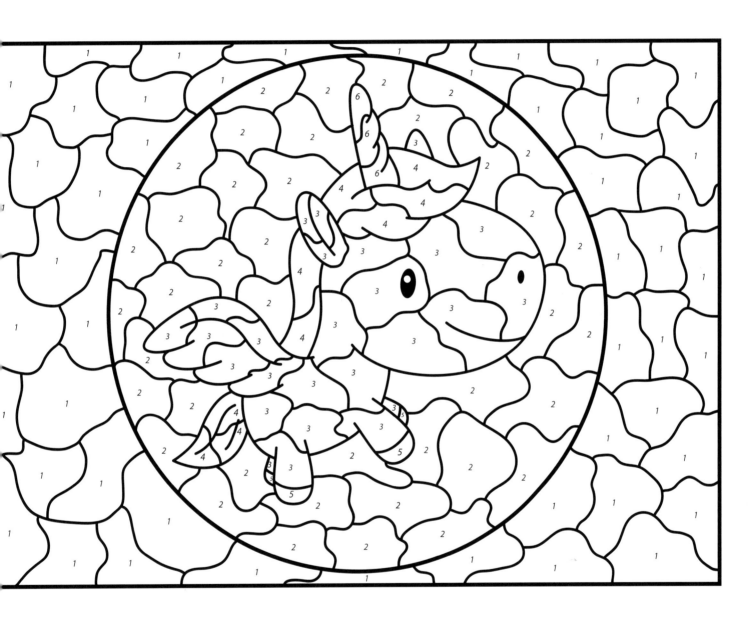

Find the right path to the crown!

CUT and GLUE

Cut and glue the image that comes next.

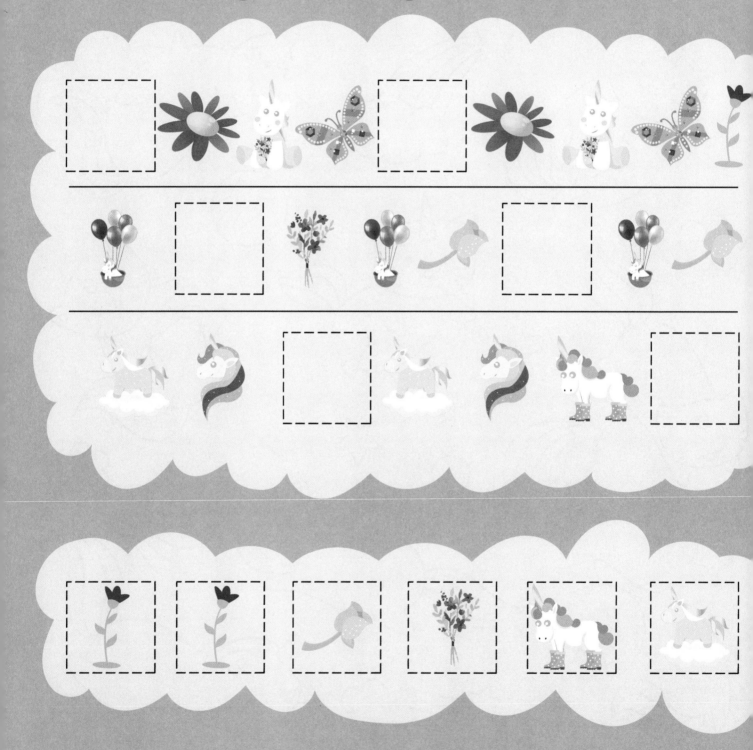

COLOR by NUMBER

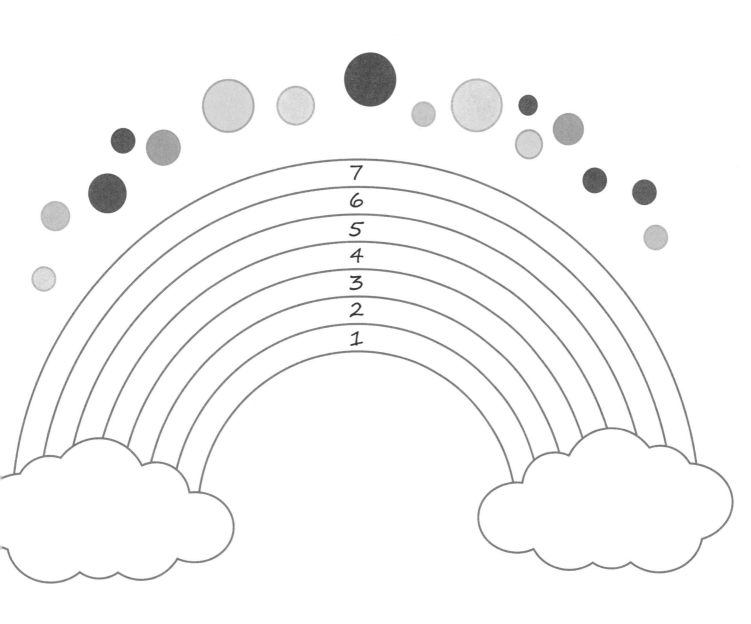

7
6
5
4
3
2
1

1 2 3 4 5 6 7

Find the right path!

Find the path to the ice cream cone by following the numbers in order.

1	2	3	4	5	6
2	1			11	12
3	14			17	18
4	20	21	22	23	24
5	6	7	8	9	10
31	32	33	34	35	11
37	38			41	12
43	44			14	13
49	50	51	52	53	54

Copy the unicorn picture one square at a time!

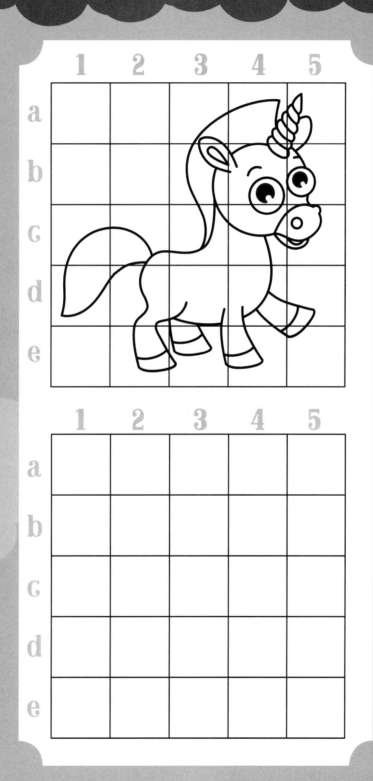

Crossword Animals

COLOR

How Many?

COUNT and COLOR

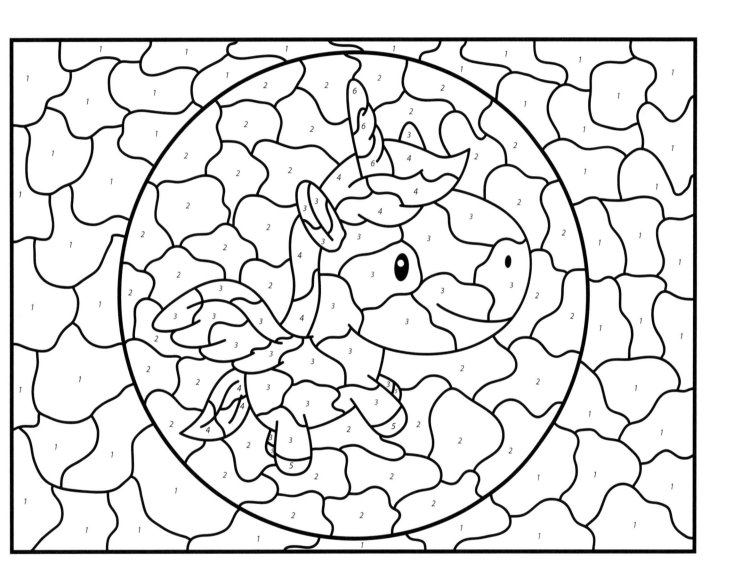

3 − 4 = ●

3 − 1 = ●

1 + 2 = ●

6 − 2 = ●

2 + 3 = ●

2 + 4 = ●

Count and write the number.

| .....Four..... | .... | .... | .... |
| .... | .... | .... | .... |

Read and Draw

| Six red balloons | Two green apples | Ten yellow circles |
| Three brown fish | Five blue stars | Eight pink flowers |

COLOR by NUMBER

Splendid Unicorns

Words that describe something are called adjectives. What adjectives come to mind when you think of a unicorn? Write them below.

SPARKLY

FUN

AMAZING

just be cool

COLOR by NUMBER

PAGE 4

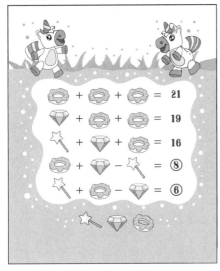

PAGE 5

PAGE 6

PAGE 8

PAGE 12

PAGE 14

		33	21	19	3	21	19	34	5	31	8
		21	7	8	16	17	34	15	37	40	
		1	4	6	8	12	30	30	34	25	17
1	16	13	4	7	16	14	17	3	28	31	5	19
21	14	31	14	10	13	16	19	22	25	33	36	38
23	27	30	21	27	35	31	21	24	25	26	27	38
19	3	25	15	21	26	2	12	2	1	33	31	30

PAGE 16

PAGE 17

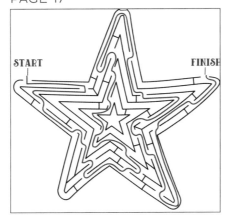

PAGE 18

PAGE 21
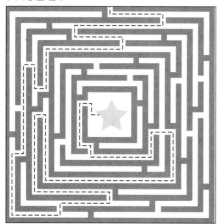

PAGE 22

PAGE 23

PAGE 24

PAGE 26
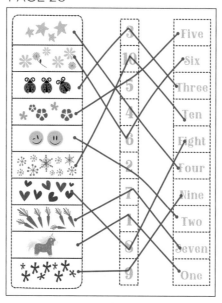

PAGE 29
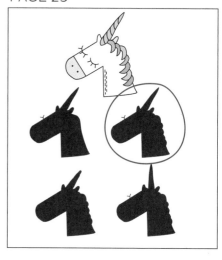

PAGE 30

PAGE 32
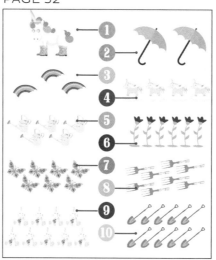

PAGE 34
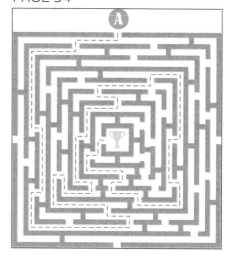

PAGE 35

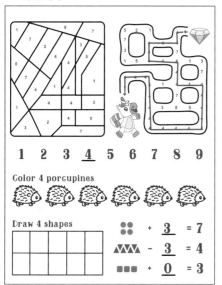

1 2 3 **4** 5 6 7 8 9

Color 4 porcupines

Draw 4 shapes

:: + **3** = 7

▲▲▲ - **3** = 4

■■■ + **0** = 3

PAGE 36

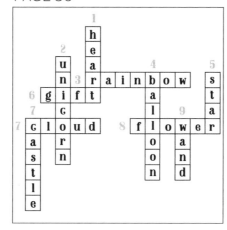

PAGE 37

PAGE 38

PAGE 39

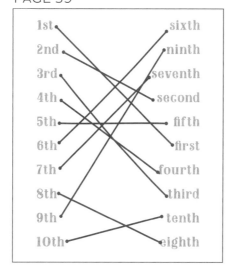

PAGE 42

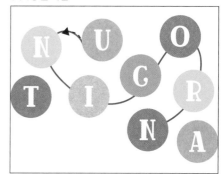

PAGE 45

PAGE 46

2	3	4	5	5	6
1	8	9	6	7	12
	15	16	8	18	
	21	10	9	24	
25	26	12	11	29	30
31	32	13	34		
37	15	14	40		
43	16	45	46	21	48
49	17	18	19	20	54

PAGE 48

PAGE 49

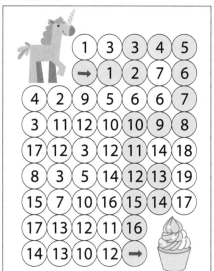

PAGE 51

PAGE 52

PAGE 54

PAGE 55

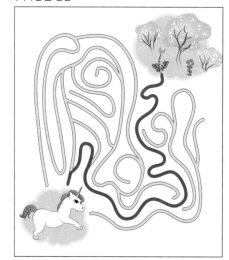

PAGE 58

PAGE 60

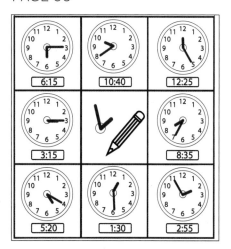

PAGE 61

PAGE 62

PAGE 63

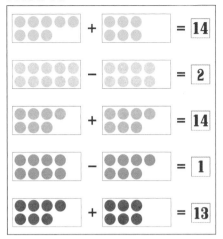

PAGE 64

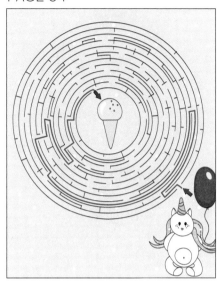

PAGE 67

PAGE 68

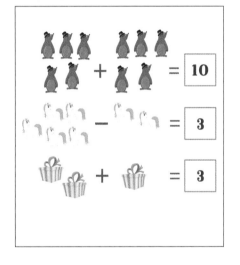

PAGE 70

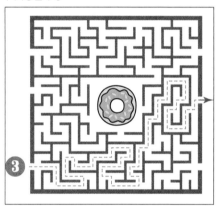

PAGE 71

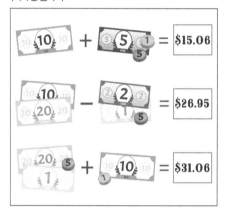

PAGE 72

PAGE 73

PAGE 74

PAGE 77

PAGE 79

PAGE 83

PAGE 84

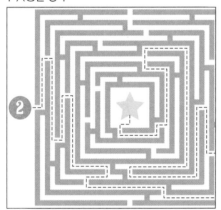

PAGE 86

PAGE 88

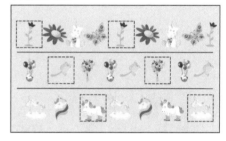

PAGE 91

PAGE 92

1	2	3	4	5	6
2	1			11	12
3	14			17	18
4	20	21	22	23	24
5	6	7	8	9	10
31	32	33	34	35	11
37	38			41	12
43	44			14	13
49	50	51	52	53	54

PAGE 94

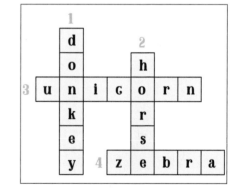

PAGE 96

PAGE 98